Down from the Sycamores

poems by

Richard Holinger

Finishing Line Press
Georgetown, Kentucky

Down from the Sycamores

ACKNOWLEDGMENTS

Merci bien! to the staffs of the following literary journals who first published
these poems:

"Four Paintings in The Louvre" in *Boulevard*
"Arcimboldo's Faces" in *Chelsea 47*
"The Sweep" in *Newsletter Inago*
"Notebook Entry on the Propagation of Sound" in *The Poetry Review*
"Detail of Holbein's *Adam and Eve*" in *Rhino*
"Fire Breather" in *Soundings East*
"*Alexander's Victory*" and "*The Plague*" in *The Texas Review*
"Dreaming of Amboise" in *Webster Review* (original title: "After Laughter")
"Ice Voices" in *Willow Review* (original title: "White Voices")

Publisher: Leah Huete de Maines
Editor: Christen Kincaid
Cover Art: Tia Holinger
Author Photo: Tia Holinger
Cover Design: Elizabeth Maines McCleavy

Order online: www.finishinglinepress.com
also available on amazon.com

Author inquiries and mail orders:
Finishing Line Press
PO Box 1626
Georgetown, Kentucky 40324
USA

Contents

For Tia, whom I love, and with whom I loved sharing many of these moments.

Part 1: Paris

Fire Breather

Before the Pompidou Center
he thickens his circle with chatter:
"Voudriez-vous voir la langue de feu?"
Francs chime on cobblestones
with increasing regularity.
Tall and emaciated,
he must not feel like eating
after tasting gasoline all day.

His pace quickens as the crowd
becomes an audience,
and he becomes a soliloquist
in a theater of the round.
His chest is hairless ivory,
his pants are black,
and he walks diameters barefoot.
Each word is crisp as kindling
even when he stoops
to pick up coins tossed as if
wishing for an accident.

He lifts the plastic bottle
like a beer and loads himself.
From the coals he takes
two glowing torches, swings them high
as an Olympic runner lighting routes,
then flattens on a blanket,
his head on a block.

He guides the first flambeau
to his mouth as if to chew,
when his lips open,
and a flame columns up

in sudden expiration.
The ring begins to splinter,
but the act is not over.

The second coal tempts
the potent mouth,
and clear fumes ignite
into blown orange breath
flaring longer than it should.
He has swilled too much,
has not emptied himself
when all his breath is gone.
He sucks fire back in
along with the air he needs.
He rolls over, pulling
the blanket with him as if
to smother lungs and throat.
He retches, coughing blood
red as liquid fire onto stones and coins.

The circle is evaporating
as he stands and shouts,
"Ce n'est rien. Ne quittez pas!"
His voice, like flint,
burns everyone it touches.

Two Bums in the Metro

Two bums heave insults back and forth
across the Metro tracks as we wait
for an Arc de Triomphe train
to take us to the Bastille Day parade.

The one on our platform speaks in outbursts,
loud, aggressive, strong, and covers two seats.
The small man on the other side
speaks quietly, incessantly, never recognizing
the presence of the other.

A blast of light explodes us
off our seats, the echo trembling farther
than anyone can see. "It is nothing,"
a passing woman in her eighties says,
"It is the Fourteenth of July. It is not
the war again." We sit down, assured
for a time it was thrown in fun,
a celebration of imitation,
and the bums keep it up.

Our train comes between them.
The large man stays in his seats,
the small man on his bench, and talk
as if they could not hear the noise.
They do not share our eagerness for parades;
they have seen such walls of men
when they were boys perched on their fathers' shoulders,
and, when older, lying on mattresses,
sleeping through sounds a hundred men make at night.

As we leave them in fluorescent light,
our screech and distance deafen us to them.
We wind through the dark to stops
that will be closed to us today.
Meanwhile, we talk about their talk,
a parade of words by two stationary men
arguing in revolutions of their own.

Parking on the *Rue de Sèze*

Ten white cars,
Mercedes, Porsches, BMWs,
park, comely as floats,
on the *Rue de Sèze*.
Beneath the dim interior lights,
blond hair drools
over smooth bends of suede skin
while fingernails long as wishes
scratch leather upholstery.

A man approaches and windows crack.
He chooses the Porsche's driver
dressed in a yellow top and white hotpants.
He talks until she lights a cigarette
and blows gray breath his way.

He returns to *La Madélèine*,
the Greek temple razed three times
and where its worshippers
once shot their priest.
Before that, Paris brought
its first trains here.
Three times he circles
this French Parthenon,
thinking of Mary Magdalen,
high-altared inside.

He knows a street
not far from *l'Opéra*
where men in animal skins
lean on cars
and ask
what time it is.

He crosses the *Marché aux Fleurs*,
silent, empty, scentless,
and walks by the delicate dishes
at *Fauchon's*: frosted turkeys,
gelled salads, layered pastries.
On walnut shelves in back sit
thirty different mustards,
pickles, and soups he once was told
he must not touch; instead, employees
would retrieve whatever he deemed
worthy of examining.

Back on the *Rue de Sèze*,
he passes up two *Citroëns*,
three Audis, and a Jaguar.
He stops beside an Alfa Romeo
where, inside, a golden Madonna
lovingly licks blood-red lips.

Part 2: The Art

The Sweep

Rising out of folding chairs beside
the *Mona Lisa*, under Titians,
along Egyptian tombs,
each skilled in remove,
leaving guarded stations,
they gather as one to close it down,
beginning at the farthest end
the sweep.

They first flow through the Grand Hall
where once a king rode horseback,
step past the headless *Winged Victory*,
brushing thousands who stayed
too long for the art,
still looking for what they'd find
if only they had time....

But now the visitors become diminished,
driven toward exits,
delivery delicate as veils
cascading down cathedral steps.

Alexander's Victory
(Albrecht Altdorfer, 1529, Alte Pinakothek, Munich)

So staged there might be a director's chair
just out of view, the artist calling, "Cut!"
Toward the end of morning's work,
the extras helmet-plumed and going limp
from holding stiff four hours' pose,
asses aching on rented mounts,
arms lanced with cramps from gripping ten-foot flags.

"Lean into it!" Altdorfer might have bull-horned
before the break, "and riders, keep your horse
positioned for a charge, forelegs reared,
or else you'll be deposed, be model for
my single casualty, the one poor bastard
symbolizing what's to come. Lunch, everyone!"

As caterers dispense white boxes
filled with bread and wine,
the painter lifts his eyes above
the castled rock, islanded lake,
and cold-blue mountain chain to pray
again for what he only had the time
to sketch before, a sky befriended with
celestial cyclone, tornadoed smoke,
and blistered clouds above a setting sun,

furious that his revisioning of death
should be in fact so hard to resurrect.

The Plague
(Arnold Böcklin, 1898, Kuntsmuseum, Basel)

It's not a good image of Death. No self-respecting
murderer would be caught dead in ponytails
riding what looks like a cross between
a pterodactyl and goose while waving *the* cliché
of kill: a long-toothed scythe.

I'll give you that he's good at leaving bodies
in his wake, the background black-clothed shadows keeling
over as if shot, the child dressed in orange
blanketing her puddled mom, another woman's back bent
back as though traversing unforgiving limbo bar,

the foreground featuring a tragedy
more narratively interesting than done-for
nobodies behind: a woman in formal blood-red dress,
hands resting over long black hair cascading
down her back, face down across the stomach
of a white-robed bride spread out on street
of jigsawed stone, thin veil spilling out
from golden hair, white-stockinged legs apart,
white-pointed shoes strapped perfectly in place.

You're just about to wonder what these two
once had in common when you spot an old man
camouflaged against the wall, his skin
and clothes the color and consistency
of what this dead, caned corpse is up against

when suddenly it dawns on you the beast
who's flying up the street, maybe right
outside your house (his black-beaked mouth still
hissing hoary frost), may not be evil after all,
his presence as inviting as the mail dropping
messages from people you've not heard from
in some time, and if you could
would like to be put back in touch with if

you only could escape this place where nothing much
is going on except the pressure to succeed,
have babies, and give pleasure to those living
next to you garaging giant self-propelled machines
that weekends fly down puzzled lanes of lawns
to mulch what little life you figure's left.

Four Paintings in The Louvre

La Radeau de Meduse (Medusa's Raft)
Theodore Gericault, 1791-1824

The foreground swells
with bodies bronzed
and ivoried, the tattered
sail labors to rescue
wind for cord-lashed logs.

Beyond, barely connected
to water so far away it seems,
a hint of a ship, hardly cause
for waving flags of shirts
and blackened arms.

Above them, continent
clouds drift, mirrors
of neglect.

Portrait de Murat roi de Naples (Portrait of Murat, King of Naples)
Antoine Jean Gros, 1771-1835

You don't see the army
until you catch the horse's wild eyes,
foaming mouth, and tiger hide
on which the gallant officer,
sword sheathed, riding in glory,
face becalmed, hangs framed,
stock-still, mount frozen
in The Louvre's hall
where a prince once galloped
in line with the Michelangelos.

La Peste d'Asdod (The Asdod Plague)
Nicolas Poussin, 1594-1665

It could be any plague
that sweeps in from the wings
where no one watching
suffering can see.

Even statues fall:
heads, hands, bases
amputated from trunks.

Only the children fail to care,
curiously eyeing what it is
that makes the old ones
feel sick about themselves.

Portrait du Peintre en chasseur (Portrait of the Painter While
Hunting)
F. Desportes, 1661-1743

The kill at his feet:
pheasant, rabbit,
and something else
too dead to tell;

Dogs pant dutifully,
the favorite patted
by its master

Who poses, head askew,
eyes on the painter,
not afraid that facing
him head-on would kill
the hunt for life.

Detail of Holbein's *Adam and Eve*
(Hans Holbein the Younger, 1517, Kunstmuseum, Basel)

Our eyes go first to her
eyes half-closed, mouth half-open.
Her cheeks, her chin, her breasts,
her fingers, all full
as Paradise.

He is dark, his eyes open, lost,
his mustache long as a secret whisper,
one arm either helping her
or holding himself up using her,
his other arm fallen
from our sight.

Their eyes do not meet,
though, like actors in a cast
whose play has closed,
each shares a part of the regret.

Our eyes finally linger
on the apple held between them
and the bruise left by a worm
into which they've bitten.

Arcimboldo's Faces
("Summer"; "Winter"; "Water"; "Fire")

They say to me
You are what you imagine:
fruit or roots, fish or flame.

Yet I also hear them whisper
that moss grows like soft hair
on the dead chins of trees,
that ripe corn should be eaten
before it hardens in the husk,
that pearls picked from forced shells
should bead around a neck,
that a pointy, black-nosed iron
could formalize a blouse.

Their vision speaks their truth:
the red-ripe cherry, knotted hole,
blowfish eye, blackened candle wick
all see more than what appears
mere forestry, glazed stare, burnt string, food;
there in all the images an apparition
is implied in the pairing of opposites,
a fruition of facing
one's worst reflection in untried glass.

But it is not what startles
that gives them away,
rather what and how they cover up:
Summer's shawl fringed and woven wheat,
Water's sea-shelled, carapace-embroidered gown,
Winter's neatly wrapped straw cloak,
Fire's pistoled, canon-barreled chest:

men tailored as destroyers and destroyed,
ravaging, rotting, finally smoldering
gracelessly to ash,
while women are robed ripe and whole,
weathering moist and warm.

Part 3: The Loire Valley

Down from the Sycamores

Down from the sycamores flaking
off the centuries, father and son
walk on cobbled ramps
that once led ships into the Loire
(given the rusted rings embedded in rock
to hold against floods certain to come).

The angle dropping, he allows the boy
to run to a rock plateau,
the promenade before the safety
of stone went up to guard Tours.
From here the son slides down
square concrete dice left over
from a bridge replaced by steel.
His father watches from the sandy bank above;
last spring he would have drowned here
as the water brought winter back to sea.

The boy drifts farther down, through snarled,
thorned berry bushes without their fruits
or bloom, through grasses water-pressed
in one direction months ago,
through sand stuccoed yesterday by rain
leaving warm mosaic prints.

He digs a hole, his throne, to watch the river,
looks up at his father, waves. The father lifts
his arm, but his son has turned to watch
anchored rowboats point upstream.

The boy calls, *"Pourquoi ne coulent-ils pas?"*
and his father tells him the weight below
the water holds them there,
each boat uses it to stay in place.

The boy asks if the chain is long enough,
how does it catch on bottoms if it stops
so near the surface? You can't see
everything, the father says. Some things
you count on to be there.
It will hold against a current
if there is anything left to unravel
should the rains lift the river.
If nothing extra, and the anchor
does not give, these things happen,
the boat goes under, becomes river, too.

He tells the boy they will return
before winter, but now he must come back
to him. The son rises, happy to be running
again in front of his father, up the ramp
to the old, ordered sycamores
spreading over the Loire.

Inlay at Chaumont

The guide describes an Aubusson tapestry,
clay medallions by Nini,
German chairbacks carved centuries before,
and a black Italian table inlaid with bone.

Whose bone? I thought, hoping
no part of me would ornament
like these bird- and shell-shaped
skeletal remains fringed nakedly
against the surrounding darkened top.

Let me instead blend into
this tapestry's soothing blues,
the once-bright woven colors
of mythology worn indistinct:

Better to hang unadorned
than to be set upon
or polished over every day.

Tapestry at Chaumont

Medusa lies prostrate in her best blue silk,
picnicking in the green town square,
her body severed at the neck
where bluish-red ribbons wave as if a fan
hidden in her heart blows forth.

To one side a soldier stands, his lance
left leaning on an apple tree
whose leaves umbrella those gathered there.
It seems he has not seen a thing,
resting like one transfixed, as though her gaze
met his while waiting there.

Around the fountain ladies wait
as if for something more, perhaps the murder
not enough, merely an hors d'oeuvre
to titillate the palette
before an entrée to war.

Flying overhead, nearly lost,
Perseus glides away on Pegasus
and holds the head
so small and plain we would think
the weaver wanted it forgotten,
like Breughel's Icarus dropped far
away, no splash to ripple lives.

And he, leaving behind statues
of men who gazed on roiling
serpentine locks, himself so near to turning
stone, fades from the center, takes flight
from shielded reflections and minutiae of life.

Dreaming of Amboise

(On the death of Charles VIII at the Chateau Amboise)

The game of fives I took the queen to watch
is still being played in the moat—
the laughs, the cheers, the taunts all
more important than the end of kings....
There are my servants, my courtiers, my wife,
my dogs. No one has come to see me die.

Why should they? Had I only nodded
when passing through the door,
I would be there, too, not staring off
this horsehair mattress edged in a corner
of Amboise I don't recognize, but rather
urging on the cheerful conflict,
feeling no more for one side than the other,
with my chateau all around me:

People, palace,
fortress I pushed up without pause:
the flame of torches made midnight day,
bonfires heated ice off winter stones
until I could fill and display this tenacious beauty
with Italian opulence and grace
never seen before in France,
Pacello bringing me even Eden
to order these gray walls above the Loire.

Such bumps as this should swell
on other heads, not those of kings
whose lives make their subjects homes.
When first I hit my head, my train looked concerned,
but I laughed it off, embarrassed I did not bend,
(should a king *ever* bend?)
perhaps too excited about getting to games,
or leaning back to better hear a lowered voice,
or dreaming of Amboise when I would be dead.

Les Oiseaux de Chenonceau

Before any of us were here,
you were here,
drafting to mosquito paths
on spread black wings
through this green forest
in circles tight and swift
as swirls in the blue Loire.

We see the need for symmetry;
we admire one thing following another
in predicted reach—walls, rocks
protect us from you who nest
in chance forks of trees.

Regardez Chenonceau: we build over
what we see, you build upon;
we part the waters by stepping in,
guide the waters by transferring them,
lift the waters by digging well into them.

But we have left you more
than your elders knew
in this southern summer home—
for even though you know ancestral
winds and rain, you now have history
in which to live, a tower
for your nests built over tourists
buying cards and slides,
from where music flows from threaded reel,
music you once heard off tightened strings,
music you once heard in the flow
of the Loire.

Part 4: Unearthed

Ice Voices
(Culled from Alfred Lansing's Endurance.*)*

The following poems describe Sir Ernest Shackleton's catastrophic 1916 expedition. His goal, to cross Antarctica, was aborted when his ship, the Endurance, *was crushed in a freak summer breeze in the Weddell Sea. After spending months on a drifting icefield, the mariners took to three small lifeboats in search of land. After several days, they landed on the tiny, remote Elephant Island. From there, Shackleton counted on tides and prevailing winds to carry him and a crew of five in the lifeboat James Caird more than 800 miles northeast to South Georgia. Arriving on the island's western side, to reach the whaling station, they crossed snow-capped mountains with only the crudest climbing equipment.*

STILL FAST

"January 24: Still fast & no sign of any opening.
"January 25: Still fast. We tried to cut away the ice, but it
was no use.
"January 28: Temperature 60 Very cold. Still fast..."
    —from the diary of Harry McNeish, carpenter of
    the Endurance

The northern winds have pushed the ice shelf
up against what land there is down here.
Here we sit, in the middle of white.

Over the next few months we try to break
through paths of water opening seductively,
then closing fast, burying our bow. The sun no
longer keeps nocturnal watch; by April first
the penguins and seals disappear, leaving us
for northern light. Dogs begin to die of worms.
By May we have only our watches to
tell time by. Night tucks us tight.

Horizon light on 26 July slits winter's
dark, but the barometer sinks past 29,
and temperatures drop to 35 below.
The blizzard blows in, punches ice
into our two-foot thick Norwegian wood.
August,

then September, whittle by as slowly
as the metal ice drives us in unfelt drift.
We write to ourselves in diaries, listen
to the phonograph screech brittle songs, and discard
greasy cards in the rathole called The Ritz.

We wait for what is building outside
To come in; who knows what it will take.
I know the screws and grains in every
beam, and yet she's more than that, now
she's pushed.

It's when the penguins come most
men give up:
ten or twelve Emperors
gather in a choral way beside
the ship, deliver song nothing like
the cheerful bracking festooned
with one another.
This is wailing, a forlorn send-off
puncturing the night like madmen
singing a requiem. McLeod murmured,
"We'll none of us get back to our homes
again." Sir Ernest bit his lip.

Those cries were worse than waking up in lantern light to
sealed walls screaming in the face of ice, worse than hearing
water pumped out the forward hold, worse than hearing men
sawing through unending rows of marble teeth that soon will
crush and swallow what's left of this tortured ship.

Our last resort, a cofferdam
I stayed up night and day to build
to bleed the sea back into sea
is finished now, just when I can tell
that nothing will hold this ocean back,
filling wherever it wishes,
crossbeams bending like bark,
and men at pumps like Hades' dead
waving farewell to well-informed Odysseus.
What pressure I hear assembling beyond
these wooden walls I love so well
I know a carpenter's tools can't touch.

ON THE ICE FLOW

"Waiting
Waiting
Waiting."
—*from Sir Ernest Shackleton's diary, January 25, 1916*

When there's nothing else to see but night and
that which crushes our *Endurance*, what once
I thought of ice is shattered,
this field of snow, slowly soaking sleeping
bags, crusting clothes, and feeding seals and dogs
to men, becomes a relentless
continent incontinent. Safe for now,
on ice as thick as inland lakes, here no help
will come. Marching lifeboats over ice-encrusted
marsh to open ocean
we know is there, but not how far,
dulls a frozen man's exhaustion raw.
Better to wait it out, better to wait
for Weddell Sea to winter north,
better to wait for the roll of the sea
beneath this land that isn't land, only
a drift of ancient seamen understanding

what they live on will someday break,
a frozen gunshot signaling icy split.
We cast off from unvarying routine
into a swelling, unkempt sea, which, compared
to this monotony of white, looks good,
until its first wave freezes into beards.

IN THE LIFEBOATS

*"Shackleton thought of the lines of Coleridge:
'Alone, alone, all, all alone,
Alone on a wide, wide sea.'"*

There's only one thing I'm afraid of:
not waves that blister
the men with cold, or oars
that freeze to gloves,
or nights so black and long that hell
would be a welcome home,
or ice we chip off
the gunwales and prow
in morning's first light,
or waterlogged food
that tastes like wood,
or ice that might
have been melted to drink;

the thing I'm afraid of
is losing each other:
out here a boat
alone is lost.

Oh, it might reach land,
some deserted scrap
of rock and ice
with pelicans and seals enough
to keep them going a year
or two.

But as long as Worsley keeps
his sextant in tune
with the sun and stars,
and currents agree with the winds,
we'll land on an island
that will hold us apart

at least from division at sea.

ELEPHANT ISLAND

"A more inhospitable place could scarcely be imagined."
—from the journal of Alexander Macklin, surgeon
of the Endurance

Shackleton didn't stay long,
left within a week, as soon as
deciding no one would
rescue us here

on this nightmare of God where
winds streak down the craggy
cliff at over a hundred knots
battering our snowbound beach,
where blizzards last days, where
leaden rocks scoff at weakened
men attempting their weight
for a shelter roofed with only
the lifeboats that someday may float
us out to die.

What life is this,
to wake up frozen every morning,
look forward to looking out
at nothing but waves a hideous gray
or icefloes luminous blue,
and never the thin, dark line
of horizon smoke?

We work to pull our eyes
from uncoming rescue: kill
penguins and seals, catch
paddies invading sea meat saved,
gather island ice melted to drink,
and talk about rescue that doesn't come
again today, about the food
our taste buds learn to ignore,
about my pulling Kerr's tooth

without deadener, about Wordie's hand
now leaking puss, Honess's sty,
and about gangrene turning
Blackboro's left foot black.

Someone tied the Royal Yacht Club flag
to an oar he buried in snow
above our camp. After dinner of penguin,
biscuits, and powdered milk, I listen
to Hussey plink on his banjo,
joined by wind fluting through cobble rock;
I can't recall last time I saw someone look up
to see if the oar was still here,
or if it had been torn free.

THE JAMES CAIRD

"May 7, 1916
54° 38' South, 39° 36' West
—from the log of Frank Worsley, captain of the
Endurance

"...a patched and battered 22-foot boat...
...her rigging festooned in a threadbare collection
of clothing and half-rotten sleeping bags..."

Eight hundred miles of ocean to cross
in twenty-two feet of lifeboat with a crew
of six who haven't bathed in over
a year and a half.

The mathematics are staggering.

"...faces were black with caked soot...
...bodies were dead white from constant soaking
in salt water...
...ugly round patches of missing skin where
frostbites had eaten into their flesh..."

I try to place us in this sea, but water
stains my books, leaves only lines enough
to acknowledge indefinite crossing.
This early morning fog unfocusses stars,
and the sea will not hold still enough for me
to read the sky. We might be nearly
there, South Georgia's western waves
that splinter boats dead ahead,
or we would be bypassing life, the tides
delivering us to thirst; it's hell not knowing
whether we'll be thrown broken
to heaven, or miss it by twenty miles.

*"...afflicted with saltwater boils on their
wrists, ankles and buttocks...
...the water brackish...polluted with
sediment and reindeer hairs..."*

If what more light brings isn't land,
and if the cormorants and seaweed never
tell us what they know, and if we have
3000 miles more of ocean emptiness,
I don't believe that even then I'll break,
not until the very end, when I lose direction
even with the sea.

SOUTH GEORGIA

*"But what if they hit a rock, Crean wanted to know....The
slope, Worsley argued. What if it didn't level off?"*

Caring about incidentals carried us this far
—to a hillside breakfast camp—
like twisting screws from gunwales
of the Caird into the soles
of our boots to catch
on mountain ice. Hard to believe
survival has come to listening
for a 7:00 a.m. start-work whistle
from the whaling station we last saw
two years ago; if we hear again
the sound I may have heard, the 6:30 wakeup
call, then home is through those two ridges
and means we've made it back.
If no whistle comes, if what
it was was only wind whipping
through the fur of my hood, or a breeze
leaking through a crevasse,
we still won't know just where
we are, won't know again
which way to take.

Worsley and Crean insisted what if:
we ran into rocks,
or a precipice ended
in nothing but air.... I said,
There's no assurance of anything here,
but imagining what a mountain can do
won't help, and the alternatives
we have are freezing here or turning back.

So we did the one thing left to us,
held onto each other,
and let go of the mountain.

Slowly we started down like an unwaxed toboggan,
but in seconds our coats froze under us
and we were skimming ice on ice
through evening light into night below,
a blackened mass of white, never any closer,
not leaning away, leaving no hints of how long
we'd fall, how many seconds, then minutes
it might be before the end,
knowing the end
might come any second, without any thoughts
of the three left on the island's west side,
or the twenty-two stranded
in the southern Atlantic—

And so we screamed,
louder than the choking wind,
lounder than our sanity could believe,
louder than what life was ever worth before.

When level finally came,
it came to us gently,
as if it knew the shock
of survival alone
could kill.

7:00 a.m. A whistle brims the eastern ridge
like a sun come out to meet three hollow men
huddled around their Primus stove.
We smile, shake hands, pick up the stove,
and go on.

Part 5: Beyond

Notebook Entry on the Propagation of Sound

(Based on the decimal system, Comte Joseph Louis Lagrange, 1736-1813, showed not only how sound was produced, but also its relation to the movement of the moon, planets, and satellites of Jupiter)

It all makes sense. It must.
From molecules pushing air
to moons parading Jupiter,
one thing holds everything
in place: space likes tens,
the answer to the universe,
easy as opening your palms
and seeing what unfolds.

Take a violin. One bow
swarms out beads of music,
impatient waves lining up
to break. Behind them:
empty space holding
nothing but history.

That's how planets and moons
corroborate. I hear them
move as in a black sea,
rolling on in decimals
of calibrated variations so fine
that even Mozart could not touch
the magic trembling through
such planetary strings.

In Appreciation

My great appreciation to Leah Huete de Maines, publisher of Finishing Line Press, for finding something in these poems worth collecting and preserving. I am grateful as well to Kevin Maines, Managing Editor, Christen Kincaid, Editor, and Mimi David for guiding me through the process to publication. Thank you, all.

Richard Holinger's short fiction, creative nonfiction, criticism, poetry, and book reviews have appeared in *The Southern Review, Boulevard, Cimarron Review, Hobart, North American Review, The Iowa Review, Witness, Chicago Quarterly Review, Chautauqua,* and elsewhere. He is a multiple Best of the Net and Pushcart Prize nominee.

About his collection of essays, *Kangaroo Rabbits and Galvanized Fences,* David Hamilton, Editor Emeritus of *The Iowa Review,* writes, "[Holinger] uses language well, has all sorts of inventive phrasing." Of *North of Crivitz,* poetry of the Upper Midwest, former Illinois Poet Laureate Kevin Stein notes, "Within these lines one hears Emerson and Frost wrestling in verdant woods." Of *Not Everybody's Nice,* winner of the 2012 Split Oak Press Flash Prose Contest, C. Michael Curtis, former Fiction Editor of *The Atlantic Monthly,* states, "their very economy and Holinger's shrewd glimpses of the human landscape make…surprisingly satisfying reading." A chapbook published by Kattywompus Press, *Hybrid Seeds: Little Fictions,* collects innovative stories published first in *Beloit Fiction Journal, Monkeybicycle, Western Humanities Review* and elsewhere. His *Thread* essay earned a "Notable" designation in *Best American Essays* 2018.

Degrees include a Ph.D. in Creative Writing from The University of Illinois at Chicago, and a M.A. in English from Washington University (St. Louis). He has taught English and creative writing on the college and secondary school levels.

New projects include a collection of creative nonfiction, *The Grounding of Flyover States,* whose pieces appeared in *Chautauqua, Catamaran, Chicago Quarterly Review, Hobart,* and elsewhere. A collection of short fiction, *Unimaginable Things,* featuring stories published in *ACM, Constellations, Gone Lawn, The Iowa Review, New Flash Fiction Review, Southern Indiana Review, Sundog, Witness,* among others, is forthcoming from Mint Hill Books. Additionally, a series of related autofictions follow his persona growing up on Chicago's Gold Coast.

Richard has two grown children, Jay and Molly, and lives with his wife, Tia, northwest of Chicago far enough to be country.

www.ingramcontent.com/pod-product-compliance
Lightning Source LLC
Chambersburg PA
CBHW020224090426
42734CB00008B/1208

* 9 7 9 8 8 9 9 9 0 0 2 2 8 *